Ca

D0617011

THE BEAUTIFUL LESSON
OF THE I

May Swenson
Poetry Award Series

THE BEAUTIFUL LESSON OF THE I

poems
by

Frances Brent

UTAH STATE UNIVERSITY PRESS
Logan, Utah

Utah State University Press
Logan, UT 84322-7800
USA

Cover art "Eagle on a Pine Tree" by Qi Baishi, Chinese: 1864–1957, *Eagle on a Pine Tree,* Hanging Scroll; ink on paper: 68 1/8 x 21 1/2 in. (173 x 54.6 cm.), detail: "The Metropolitan Meseum of Art, Gift of Robert Hatfield Ellsworth, in memory of La Ferne Hatfield Ellsworth, 1986. (1986.267.216) Photograph © 2000 The Metropolitan Museum of Art"
Cover design by Barbara Yale-Read
Manufactured in the United States of America

The following poems have appeared in earlier versions in the journals cited. Many thanks to their editors and publishers:
  The Denver Quarterly: "Little Dream Before Sleep," "Blisters," "Star," and "Snow with the Cat"
  New American Writing: "Porcelain Blue Boat," "Lampholder and Bucket," and "The Beautiful Lesson of the I"
  The New Yorker: "The Rat"
  The Notre Dame Review: "The Silver Skates," "Figure and Moth," and "Man and Demons"
  Web Conjunctions: "Angel" and "Vagabond"
  The Yale Review: "Fire in the Doll's House"

Library of Congress Cataloging-in-Publication Data

Brent, Frances Padorr.
The beautiful lesson of the I : poems / by Frances Brent.
    p. cm. -- (May Swenson Poetry Award series)

    ISBN 0-87421-616-8 (alk. paper)

    I. Title. II. Series.
    PS3602.R457B43 2005

                                        2005014247

*For Jonathan
and to Ben, Jesse, and Jennie*

CONTENTS

PART TWO *The Box*

ACKNOWLEDGMENTS

Portions of this book received recognition from the Poetry Society of America, for which I am truly thankful. I am grateful as well to the many journals that published first versions of my poems, sometimes under different titles; they are acknowledged on the copyright page.

Several poems in this collection were inspired by paintings and drawings. I want especially to acknowledge my debt to the following artists: Hsia Kuei: *The Clear and Sonorous Air of the Fisherman's Flute;* Vermeer: *View of Delft;* Qi Baishi: *Insects and Plants;* Corrot: *Port de La Rochelle;* Giorgio Morandi, *Bottles;* Bada Shanren, *Hen and Chick;* Picasso, *Seated Harlequin;* Watteau, *Gilles;* Rene d'Anjou, *King Rene's Book of Love;* James Ensor, *Candle and Bucket, Hands, Peculiar Insects, House with Puppets,* and *The Strike or Massacre of the Ostend Fishermen.*

My title, *The Beautiful Lesson of the I,* is borrowed from Ensor's enigmatic and visionary *Mes ecrits.*

Lines quoted in "Fire" are taken from Anna Sewell's *Black Beauty.* "Bleeding Heart" was suggested by several of the lyrical and erotic poems in Huynh Sanh Thong's *An Anthology of Vietnamese Poems.* The title "Memory is the Treasure House of all Things" should be attributed to Marcus Tullius.

As the pun in its title reminds us, this collection is full of poems about seeing. But since, appropriately for the distilled and trenchant character of this book, no word in the title is inert, the poems in "The Beautiful Lesson" are also about beauty (a word for which I find no good synonym) and about teaching and learning.

A primary lesson these poems teach: pay attention. The physical smallness of most of them on the page works to focus eye, ear, and mind (and this modest scale, I can't resist adding, is a welcome contrast to the many poems one sees these days whose heedless expanses tax the attention of the most sympathetic reader by attempting narrative dimensions without providing the pleasures of narrative). But the ambition in these very un-narrative poems is far from miniature. The fact that we need to lean in close to catch what is being said does not mean that the book is a catechism of diminutives. Yes, a walnut, an apple, a doll's house, a rat, an egg are all small—but small compared to what? All are larger than what they contain, and they all contain something. I am reminded of Hamlet's claim that he could be bounded in a nutshall and count himself a king of infinite space, "were it not that I have bad dreams." In "The Beautiful Lesson of the I," both space and dreams figure. The rat's carcass turns out to contain "disquieting continents"; the basket, the bottle, the box, and most notably the globe are all vessels. "Globe," which provides a witty and original evocation of a floating fetus, speaks of "the substanceless / envelope where something is preserved / but made small enough to go unnoticed." That envelope might contain pickling fluid, an embryo, or a poem.

As students of fermentation know, inseparable from preservation is transformation—and transformation in poetic terms is trope. "Melon," a poem to which I kept returning, begins "There once was a man / who had to see everything in order to remember." "See" here turns out to mean something akin to "liken to something else," for what follows is as vivid and accurate a rendition of a melon rind (cantaloupe, I think) as I've ever come across: "the melon is a grained and dented moon covered in netting." Exactly. Or in "Rose," which can hardly help evoking Blake in passing, "A finger-sized hole / bores through the outspread folds / like a cigarette burn. / When I turn back the petals, / I uncover the silver, jeweled beetle."

The rightness and precision in poem after poem here correspond to and are buttressed by the quiet authority of a voice that issues from painstaking observation, not improvisation and anecdote. Nor is the observation limited to the phenomenal world, for poems like "Little Dream before Sleep" and "The Place Where I Harbor Anger" contrive to make visible intensely inward and private, yet also surely universal, experiences.

The beautiful lesson of this quiet and unerring book is above all mimesis—not merely in the sense of *A* resembling *B,* but in the much more untamed sense of correspondences that can be unexpected, grotesque, or sinister. No wonder James Ensor is a presiding presence here—but (among others) so too, it occurs to me, is May Swenson, whose poetry has some of the same homely yet *unheimlich* character, some of the same patient attention which never feels humdrum but rather leans toward defamiliarization, and some of the wonder and delight that is offered by "The Beautiful Lesson of the I." And though I hadn't taken this into account while making my choice among competing manuscripts, I believe Swenson would have admired and enjoyed this collection—as I do.

Rachel Hadas

THE BEAUTIFUL LESSON
OF THE I

PART ONE
The Clear and Sonorous Air

THE CLEAR AND SONOROUS AIR

section of a handscroll, Southern Sung Dynasty

Homeless spirit, breath
drifts   this inkblot   milky cliffs
my small, sorry heart.

THE SILVER SKATES

In the remnant world, across half-frozen canals,
even the draft horses were lifted upon wide wooden stools.
Swans hugged the glass collar of a sawed off ice block;
hills of bare, pendant branches enclosed the painted water like a net.

I am skating on this unfinished lens,
balancing my weight against its plate of metal.

Who sweeps that green
rim with the marvelous, polishing wheel,
bathing its stained edges
in the jeweler's wooden bucket
of ice-water?

DELFT

If I could release my eye
from the gabled roofs and wooden sheds,
that terrestrial belt across the canal—

Memory landscape lies oxidized over the ale-colored water—
Over the ale-colored water, the filament of my double selves
lies cradled in smallest proportion.

PORT DE LA ROCHELLE

Composed out of the filings of gold and ivory,
miniature turbaned figures collect by the stone embankment:
A laborer unpacks his donkey, another rolls his barrel,
the docksman lowers his wooden pole to water in the cove—

And this is the moment just after commotion
when the beech trees are ragged and tall plaster houses
stack about like cartons.
The eavesdropper, shielded in the window above the seawall,
pauses in a particle of ecstasy before continuing
thought to its vanishing point.

In the next life, what does
a donkey become?

PLATE AND INSECT

Hunger, a fume in the rice-colored nothingness
surrounds the empty dish
and an insect, the shape of a watermelon seed,

and then evaporates.

My serenity
rests in the invisible scale pan, then moves freely
between the immaculate ringed plate

and back to the small, black smear with flecks
for legs, between an oval
drawn on paper and the dark puddle

of little Buddha in tails,
a cockroach and its porcelain nest,
clump of brush hair

and the imagined heaviness of the Chinaman's
unreal bowl, God's mouth
and potbellied air.

I live between two things,
the stoniness of the open and the other
filled with gold,

fullness
and a pebble.
I disperse into a cloud of raw milk.

LITTLE DREAM BEFORE SLEEP

Sketches of a lathered
fallen horse.

The flower's brooding stamen swims
unclouded in its bell-shaped cup.

I can trace the bloodshot crack
in his white organ of sight.

Etchings, etchings and line.

LAMPHOLDER AND BUCKET

Arch of the carved wooden bedframe
iron coated bucket
lampholder
guttered candle
narrow black box
handpuppet   *with the face of a pig*

Beneath beautiful objects
lie the empty outlines of your hands

the patience of things.

ANGEL

Swarming the angel's hair which is substanceless
and from his body to the seams of his mesh clothes,
the lice crawl to the bladder of his genitals
and past his womanly mouth.

He has that dazed look, half-opportunist, half-lamb,
of all the other angels.

While they travel so lightly
along his wax hand, they drink from his deprivation.

APPLE

Here's the cross-section of apple, seed house, stem,
ink on its membrane scraped with a knife. And here's the walnut,
little foreign heart, withered vein, shell where meat
lies burrowed
      incubus in a dark soul.
And the burial mound—
spiral that was human   violet   clay pot
round as an apple.

BLEEDING HEART

from the Vietnamese

Little, red pitcher, partially filled with water—
stretched, ticking, three-cornered as my purse—

Then waterless,
shredded,
faded, purple—
red.

BLISTERS

The blisters are cloth bells in air,
small, aggrieved flowers

filled with sugar of fingertips,
they open in their time.

Bedraggled scarabs,
blood symbols of the days

are stamped to their underbellies
like fat colophons.

They are the lilies
and flies that settle on marble,

sticking to gauze like honey,
churning unmerited purity.

BOTTLES

The bottles stand like empty houses
little sloped earthmounds
pale loaves on an uneven field

necks taper
into rice colored chimneys
and all of the sediment is paint.

BUTTERFLY

The butterfly is formed out of the same nothingness
as the tree or ragged horse.
Its spots are cinders of glazed copper.
Its veins converge over the powdered
surface like folds of a fan.

Now, it is a little tent balanced on my finger,
the undersides paler than a torn Japanese umbrella.

CAGE

The cage fills completely,
the charcoal goat passes through its needle,
through its window bars, pipe steam,
hill of black soot.

And in the cricket box
there are fifty-four dowel pins that sound
like the tubes of a wooden xylophone
when I strike them with
my finger.

CORPSE

Unmitigated
suffering
is transformed
to beautiful
pen line:

the knuckles of the blindman's hand,
for instance.

Loneliness is absorbed like the transpiration of water
through grass.

Balance
is found
in emptiness
surrounding
every
pigmentless
element.

DOG

The staves of a dog's ribs are rounded, surrounding
breath and the essence of breath

is indifference—
> *The dog has the face of a doe*
> *mouthing ascendancy, pricking knuckles with the crushed glass*
of its milk teeth.

Disturbance runs along the curve of the shoulder,
shining, black hindquarters.

Anguish is the rope tied to the throat.

Star is strapped to the forechest.

EGG

The egg is decorating itself with gold.
The gold, gliding around the surfaces,
becoming ready for its own unwinding.

EGGS IN A BASKET

Those eggs aren't large and cold or white
as the two I hold in my hand,
but speckled brown or painted like the five

blue eggs in the antique dealer's sunken stall.
Gilded hair's breadth cracks are strung
along the surfaces of shell.

FIGURE AND MOTH

The Dutch painters record how the pupil of the eye
accommodates to the candle's crack of light at the door:
burnished-brown miniature cloud
surrounding the miniature gold crown
of the tallow.

Distortion resides in ever-dissolving form:
the impostor appears at a well-pump;
his flaxen limbs relax
after the hosen are unraveled.

Someone with perfect brush stroke
must catch this meal moth
circling his incandescence,
down to its dull scales
and powder.

FIRE

lines from a children's book

Horses rear and stumble, farmers burn their hands on lead rope,
dragging them blindfolded through sickening fog—
When legs of the field horses buckle,
the beasts are wound in gold and suffocating—
a legion of agonized and rusting animals:

"There was a dreadful sound
before we got into our stalls, the shrieks of those poor horses
that were left burning to death in the stable—it was very terrible!"

Horses burnished by the fire, to the fire it's immaterial.

FIRE IN THE DOLL'S HOUSE

The paper house ignites
with an alchemist's bellows.

Golden-finned, arched, dying, re-aroused,
encircling every human and thimble-sized object—

Love, with the tiniest, red torch branded to your heart—
will you come now?

Blood blooms lie decked on the mounted beams,
devouring the scabs of tissue roses.

They follow the crumb paths
through little halls and rooms

no larger than the width of a child's hand:
tablets for worms, baskets for a litter of mice,

gnats swim in the pool
of a toy teacup—

Inside the sleeping tents,
vapor unwinds the dolls from the dolls' beds.

Acid   ash   snowcloud
little white sails.

GLOBE

I am trying to loosen the miniature globe
that is grafted at my waist.
It is lighter than the smallest drop of water

even as it increases to the size of a balloon,
it will out-grow my middle
like the acorn of a uterus with channels

and rivers to feed the weightless embryo
lodged in its pastel-colored cartouche,
moving slightly, left to right

like shifting water, thoughtfully,
but in air; it reminds me of a Japanese lantern
stretching out of crepe paper

and drenched rags, webbed
into film of a porous cloud,
or a toy moon with puckered landmasses

stirred from the substanceless
envelope where something is preserved
but made small enough to go unnoticed.

HARLEQUIN

Propped on the board by the flat
Of his fish-shaped hands,

weightless
inside the diamond of his trunk,

the boy harlequin's released—

Marvel at the mourning
on his nicked-out face,

excavated remains
of his presence.

HEART WITH METAL CORDS

Illumined heart,
painted with blood and inscribed in *The Book of Love*—

where Coeur was blindfolded
but encased in metal,

emblem of love
punched on his silver shield.

The ink of the block-pressed fleurons,
was drawn by the master

from the valves of a cow,

but in the dream
it was made from iron or silver—

the heart with metal cords.

HEN AND CHICK

The huge black hen
almost covers the chick completely.

She brings his soul to her imaginary rooms
so it won't become lost.
At first he's hungry,
entering the cage of her Chinese silk
and she warms him with her mouth,
iron folds, her mountain
flesh. And when it becomes
hard to bear
he settles into the emptiness.

HORSE

Muscles strap about floundering legs,
the barrel of his chest—
the skull, long, solemn, vacant, concentrates
on the fly dropping eggs
into the warm slab of his turd.
When he gallops, I pump the burden of his girth. Hooves
slogging mud become the spongy
flow of blood through the heart's valve.
Afterwards, I put my face
to the iridescent horseflesh.

INFANT

The sagging skin of the infant
hangs on its skeleton
like folds of worn burlap.
A knee bends in an athlete's pose
and the colorless organs
bulge beneath the flower.

MAN AND DEMONS

He drew whimsical soldiers
with escape in mind.

Lowered his sleeve to the latticed
skin of a pond.

The heart beneath his burlap shirt
grew inflamed in grief.

In pity the armature of Love
was severed from his volatile conscience.

A spirit presented the gouge of ear stumps,
egg of a face.

Bells were played
by the one with black teeth.

Ghosts took their place
in tapestry gardens.

MELON

There once was a man
who had to see everything in order to remember:

The melon is a grained and dented moon covered in netting—

helmet with shallow ridges
for the finger to travel across its pucker—

salmon-red
bladder
of seed, lopsided
dream-
face.

THE PLACE WHERE I HARBOR ANGER

I'm in a miniature sailboat:
the sea is shallow,
the air pellucid.
I can smell the green grass
coloring the base of a scallop shell.
It sways gently out of perspective
and no one can hear for the shouting.

PORCELAIN BLUE BOAT

Nothing is this water
broken by my eagerness.

Tangled string
    now what have I done?

Silence engine
at the bottom of the glass.

Flat
tin voice
of the deaf.

The mountain is a mirror of the stranger's anatomy,
the organs roped together.

Drooping pines at the base form a canopy
for the traveler the size of a dot
and the rocks and damp wooden steps
are drawn with the same pen lines
as the waffle pattern of the velvet clusters of moss.

At the top, where it rains,
everything is scratched out.

THE RAT

Not the dapper
bespectacled little grandfather
with quilted silk coat and leather boots

but the long-tailed, appallingly limp
carcass left by the cat in freezing wind.
Neck twisted like a cleaning rag,
mouth leaking syrup,
bead-glass eyes of a doll—

And here are the diligent maggots
scrambling over disquieting continents.

ROSE

In the notebook, the rose
is a vortex of lines, curls
on a wounded gray skull.

But, in the garden,
it is red velvet,
gold sewn thriftily at the center.

A finger-sized hole
bores through the outspread folds
like a cigarette burn.

When I turn back the petals,
I uncover the silver, jeweled beetle.

SCISSORS

Without much attention,
I slip on the rings of the scissors
and work in the poor light of the kitchen.
The blades chomp at the cloth
I hold in my hand.
Upstairs the night is stale
as this cup of water.

SHELLS

In winter you can blow into them like God's horn:
Some are ivory vagabonds with chafed limbs.

The fat, bodiless infant star
tumbles its reincarnation before the rotation

of the planets.
          Sea horses slice
paper warriors on wooden sticks.

When you turn over the leopard conch,
you see it's a house with nothing much to do inside.

SNOW WITH THE CAT

First it's pollen, or the drug
shaken down from the sides of this glass;
then ravens shoot across the yard:
Powder shot off Baroque Actaeon's Baroque bow—

Now he's licking his paws clean,
licking each pocket of claw.

STAR

Dusty and enormous planet—
dull, wooden ball swooping the road—

Rings start up—
chafe with colossal effort.

In the window, there's the glint
left from a hairbrush.

THUNDERMOUTH

a hand puppet

My hand fits inside the open gray house
of his body.

My thumb and fingers poke bashfully
through the rag hollow.

That is my pointer in the tunnel that leads
to the lopsided mass of his plaster head,

his face, the pencil and water marks
rubbed at the corner,

unrepaired cowlick, clouded
and wandering blue-white of his eyes—

Here is the shapeless messenger
at the immense door

I will open quietly.

TREE

The tree is a stick with two lines,
a triangle

of the lungs releasing breath.
It is a blot of ink

where the homunculus begins his journey
over the mountains,

or comes to rest in the darkness
under the ballast.

VAGABOND

He stumbles as he gets off the train,
clothes corroded with acid from the cakes of dirt he would alchemize.

He has the jagged profile
of the draftsman's toothless shepherd.

And, when he speaks, you will hear the gravel
clanking in his throat—

The fusion of metal in this old coin is nothing
to that alloy of pulverized charcoal and aniseed.

PART TWO
The Box

THE BOX

The box comes in a dream, the one painted indigo,
with the little broken tray and broken message.

GHOST CAT

The crook of his gray feathers
release to earth.

I look for the coil—
little muscles of abdomen—

Ghost cat sinks in
the way cutouts disappear
on the painted dish
with delicacies

the way I wish to thank
down-in-the-
soil.

RELIC DREAM

Wading in a shallow crook of the river,
pilgrims surround the relic raised on a palanquin—
It's a fine piece of carved wood, oiled, perfumed,
full of weight, shaped roughly like a human foot
or phallus—

a wooden boat—that's how to bathe a god,
gently and solemnly, the way to bathe an infant,
for the first time in the object world. But a boat
will drift over water, shoe-shaped, at the start of a journey,
float like a suitcase.

THEATRICAL OF CLOWNS

Children's musical cylinders revolve and the circus troop gathers
in the natural light of the garden.
Characters assemble, wearing stiff white collars of rococo clowns.
Pierrot is pulled into the sweetened middle, surrounded by ornamental
trees and shrubs.
Sea rhythms scoop against the bedlam.

Columbine (glancing at the red and white painted clown):
 "I don't know what to do!
I've pushed that garlanded mule as far as he'll go!"

Harlequin bashes Pierrot
with a wooden stick.

Wrapped in his loneliness,
Pierrot rolls on the ground like an egg.

Before lighting his gunpowder, Punchinello
leaps in a series of hand-flips: *"I'll ruin the lot of you!"*

The air fills with alternating bells of finger cymbals.
"How will you transform that restlessness into beauty?" asks Mouse.

OLD STORY FROM THE HOUSE WITH PUPPETS

Exhumed from darkness, the ancient marionettes rotate on hangers
strung from the rooftops of the tall houses.
Weighted with sawdust, they're immense and floundering.

The dancer on tiptoe presents the rose of her sexuality.

Jack-in-the- box leers, *Have the goodness, here's the goblet!*
    Keep your eye-blobs to yourself!

A vagabond and, afterward, soft gray sewer rats pursue the one-legged
    soldier until the drooping
sides of his paper boat slip through the grates of a culvert and he is
    followed by the horn-scaled
fish, tail streaming like an underwater kite, who swallows him.

Then the beloved is arranged
in the weighted sleep of a banquet
fish—on a platter.

Three chimerical figures: dragonfly, beetle, cockroach,
each with a human head.
Setting: Far behind them, an uncut field and a wooden house.
A little man leans from the window.
Stage effects: Wind sifts through etched clouds.
Choppy rumbles in the bass.
Quiet and repeated broken chords for melody.
Grave serenade.

Narrator (Pointing to the slightly smudged image in drypoint):
Notice how the insect, with its exterior skeleton, approaches real form.

The dragonfly poses in cameo and the beetle gazes straight ahead
with mustachioed expression of tension.

The cockroach (crying, he is a protesting baby): *Wahhhh!*

The beetle (speaking to the dragonfly in his lowest voice*)*:
I don't believe I can trust anyone with my solitary thoughts.

Narrator: *Notice the cage of the beetle's abdomen.*

The dragonfly (she is slightly agitated):
But I woke you from an exhausting dream.

The Beetle (his voice, again, is very low):
I'm sorry, here is my broken face. I don't want to talk.

The cockroach (his mouth open wide): *Wahhhh!*

The dragonfly (just remembering):
I want to find beauty in nothingness.
In The Doctrine of Emptiness there is no eye.

Narrator: *One must put art where it belongs.*

Hundreds of characters: bare chested men with banners and effigies, wailing women, rioting children, flying spirits, soldiers, skeletons, horses, dogs, vomited fish and rotting eels.

Setting: The scene is shaped horizontally in layers, part carnival, part apocalypse. Atmosphere of a toy theater with skirmishes on the street and pandemonium in the galleries. Smoke, Chinese kites, baskets, fish net, balloons, gold and rose-colored fog.

Stage effects: Candle for smoke, toy guns and gun powder when rifles discharge, a large fan creates the noise of wind.

Music: drums, penny whistles, shooting

As the curtain rises, there is shouting and moaning, all speaking at once. Some are vomiting, some throwing piss pots, soldiers curse.

The Fisherman's Wife rages at a Soldier but the Soldier is shut up in his own confusion.

Little Man in the Upper Gallery (he's pushing the head of another man into a basket): *Revenge!*

Thoughts of the Fisherman's Wife: *I cut the fish and the fish heads as though they were melons.*
They floated in water.

Soldier: *She's kicking the empty bucket!*

Child in the Street: *Now we're lost.*
I don't recognize any of these faces or buildings.

Narrator (pointing left and right): *Do you see how it's possible to change, but perhaps not completely?*
Can you see the feather lurking in the fish bones?

UNDO

I drew a finger through the air with its memory objects—
there's nothing
but there is. I leaned the gray word
against the wall with the clock

and the dark compositions of *Prohibition* and *Desire*,
space between thought going off
and coming back—

Undo—
choppy feeling of the heart—
so much hope
as the bubble floats.

MEMORY IS THE TREASURE HOUSE OF ALL THINGS

I have a miniature, silver shovel to push the apples—*words*—across
    the plate.
Commotion floats safely beyond the small portions.

Plaster cakes are carried by diminutive figures with turbans
and silk robes who unwrap the tumbling papers, paintings

or handwriting interrupted by stars and geese. Sometimes
I let my eyes wander across the four landscapes,

borrowed ideas about emptiness, balance, longing, passing time.
Familiar feelings encumber me while I concentrate.

Frances Brent was born in Chicago and was educated at Barnard College. She studied poetry at Columbia University and the University of Illinois, Chicago. She has taught courses at Yale, Loyola University, Northwestern University, and Barat College. From 1984 to 1991 she co-edited the literary journal, *Formations*. In 1987 she co-translated *Beyond the Limit, Poems by Irina Ratushinskaya*. She lives with her family in New Haven.

THE MAY SWENSON
POETRY AWARD

This annual competition, named for May Swenson, honors her as one of America's most provocative and vital poets. In the words of John Hollander, she was "one of our few unquestionably major poets." During her long career, May was loved and praised by writers from virtually every major school of poetry. She left a legacy of nearly fifty years of writing when she died in 1989.

May Swenson lived most of her adult life in New York City, the center of American poetry writing and publishing in her day. But she is buried in Logan, Utah, her birthplace and hometown.